BASEBALL LEGENDS

Hank Aaron
Grover Cleveland Alexander
Ernie Banks
Johnny Bench
Yogi Berra
Roy Campanella
Roberto Clemente
Ty Cobb
Dizzy Dean
Joe DiMaggio
Bob Feller
Jimmie Foxx
Lou Gehrig
Bob Gibson
Rogers Hornsby
Reggie Jackson
Walter Johnson
Sandy Koufax
Mickey Mantle
Christy Mathewson
Willie Mays
Stan Musial
Satchel Paige
Brooks Robinson
Frank Robinson
Jackie Robinson
Babe Ruth
Tom Seaver
Duke Snider
Willie Stargell
Honus Wagner
Ted Williams
Carl Yastrzemski
Cy Young

BASEBALL LEGENDS

BABE RUTH

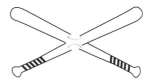

Norman L. Macht

Introduction by
Jim Murray

Senior Consultant
Earl Weaver

CHELSEA HOUSE PUBLISHERS
New York • Philadelphia

ACKNOWLEDGMENTS

This story could not have been told as completely and accurately without the generous help of everyone at the Babe Ruth Museum in Baltimore; Mrs. Mary Moberly, Babe Ruth's sister; and Lori Rader of the Wilmington Institute Library.

Published by arrangement with
Chelsea House Publishers.
Newfield Publications is a federally
registered trademark of Newfield
Publications, Inc.

Produced by James Charlton Associates
New York, New York.

Designed by Hudson Studio
Ossining, New York.

Typesetting by LinoGraphics
New York, New York.

Picture research by Carolann Hawkins
Cover illustration by Dan O'Leary

Library of Congress Cataloging-in-Publication Data

Macht, Norman L. (Norman Lee) , 1929-
    Babe Ruth / Norman Macht ; introduction by Jim Murray ; senior consultant Earl Weaver.
        p. cm.
    Includes bibliographical references and index.
        Summary: Presents the life and career of George Herman Ruth, perhaps the most talented and popular player in baseball history.
    ISBN 0-7910-1189-5. — ISBN 0-7910-1223-9 (pbk.)
    1. Ruth, Babe, 1895-1948—Juvenile literature. 2. Baseball players—United States—Biography—Juvenile literature. [1. Ruth, Babe, 1895-1948. 2. Baseball players.] I. Title.
GV865.R8M331991   [92]90-47186
796.357'092—dc20   CIP
[B]   AC

CONTENTS

WHAT MAKES A STAR

Jim Murray

No one has ever been able to explain to me the mysterious alchemy that makes one man a .350 hitter and another player, more or less identical in physical makeup, hard put to hit .200. You look at an Al Kaline, who played with the Detroit Tigers from 1953 to 1974. He was pale, stringy, almost poetic-looking. He always seemed to be struggling against a bad case of mononucleosis. But with a bat in his hands, he was King Kong. During his career, he hit 399 home runs, rapped out 3,007 hits, and compiled a .297 batting average.

Form isn't the reason. The first time anybody saw Roberto Clemente step into the batter's box for the Pittsburgh Pirates, the best guess was that Clemente would be back in Double A ball in a week. He had one foot in the bucket and held his bat at an awkward angle—he looked as though he couldn't hit an outside pitch. A lot of other ballplayers may have had a better-looking stance. Yet they never led the National League in hitting in four different years, the way Clemente did.

Not every ballplayer is born with the ability to hit a curveball. Nor is exceptional hand-eye coordination the key to heavy hitting. Big-league locker rooms are filled with players who have all the attributes, save one: discipline. Every baseball man can tell you a story about a pitcher who throws a ball faster than anyone has ever seen but who has no control on or *off* the field.

The Hall of Fame is full of people who transformed themselves into great ballplayers by working at the sport, by studying the game, and making sacrifices. They're overachievers—and winners. If you want to find them, just watch the World Series. Or simply read about New York Yankee great Lou Gehrig; Ted Williams, "the Splendid Splinter" of the Boston Red Sox; or the Dodgers' strikeout king Sandy Koufax.

A pitcher *should* be able to win a lot of ballgames with a 98-miles-per-hour fastball. But what about the pitcher who wins 20 games a year with a fastball so slow that you can catch it with your teeth? Bob Feller of the Cleveland Indians got into the Hall of Fame with a blazing fastball that glowed in the dark. National League star Grover Cleveland Alexander got there with a pitch that took considerably longer to reach the plate; but when it did arrive, the pitch was exactly where Alexander wanted it to be—and the last place the batter expected it to be.

There are probably more players with exceptional ability who didn't make it to the major leagues than there are who did. A number of great hitters, bored with fielding practice, had to be dropped from their team because their home-run production didn't make up for their lapses in the field. And then there are players like Brooks Robinson of the Baltimore Orioles, who made himself into a human vacuum cleaner at third base because he knew that working hard to become an expert fielder would win him a job in the big leagues.

A star is not something that flashes through the sky. That's a comet. Or a meteor. A star is something you can steer ships by. It stays in place and gives off a steady glow; it is fixed, permanent. A star works at being a star.

And that's how you tell a star in baseball. He shows up night after night and takes pride in how brightly he shines. He's Willie Mays running so hard his hat keeps falling off; Ty Cobb sliding to stretch a single into a double; Lou Gehrig, after being fooled in his first two at-bats, belting the next pitch off the light tower because he's taken the time to study the pitcher. Stars never take themselves for granted. That's why they're stars.

1

THE SUPER SOUTHPAW

Mention the name Babe Ruth, and everyone immediately thinks of home runs. In 22 seasons of major league play, he walloped an amazing 714 of them. Over the years, millions of fans turned out to watch the Babe take his mighty swing. They hoped to see him hit one of those long, high drives that seemed to scrape the sky and defy gravity before it plummeted down into the bleachers.

But with all his thunderous hitting, Babe Ruth's proudest moments came not in the batter's box but on the mound.

He broke into the major leagues as a pitcher with the Boston Red Sox in 1914 and quickly became the best lefthander in the American League.

The Red Sox won the pennant in his first full season, 1915, but Ruth did not get to pitch in the World Series. His team won again in 1916, and this time he started the second game against the Brooklyn Dodgers. The first batter he faced hit an inside-the-park home run. That might have rattled any 21 year old making his World Series

Ruth quickly established himself as one of the best lefthanded pitchers in the American League.

debut, but young Babe Ruth kept his composure.

The Red Sox tied the game in the 3rd inning, and Ruth kept mowing down the Dodgers. Unfortunately, the Dodger pitcher, Sherry Smith, was doing the same thing to Boston. The two hurlers matched zeroes into the 10th, 11th, 12th, and 13th innings. By that time it was getting dark, and because no ballparks in America had lights yet, the umpires almost called the game. But they decided to play one more inning.

In the last of the 14th, Boston scored a run to win the longest World Series game ever played. After giving up five hits in the 1st inning, Ruth had held the Dodgers scoreless for the last 13.

Two years later, in 1918, American soldiers were deep in the muddy trenches of Europe fighting in World War I. Because baseball was not considered essential to the war effort, the government cut short the season and had it end on Labor Day. Ruth won 13 and lost 7 as the Red Sox captured another pennant.

The super southpaw was named to pitch the Series opener against the Chicago Cubs on September 5th. The Cub pitcher was another southpaw, a big veteran named Hippo Vaughn. Boston scratched out one run off him in the 4th inning, and that was all they could manage. But it was enough for Ruth, who gave up only 6 singles to gain a 1–0 victory. He had now blanked National League batters for 22 straight innings in World Series play.

Contrary to his appearance in pictures taken when he was older, Babe Ruth was not always built like a barrel. At 23, he was 6 feet, 2 inches tall, strong, trim-waisted, and fast. He was also wild and boisterous, a fun-loving kid who would never grow up. On the train ride from Chicago to Boston after game 1, the playful Babe got into a friendly scuffle with another player and scraped the knuckles of his pitching hand against the steel wall of the railroad car. By the next morning, his middle finger had swollen to twice its normal size.

Ruth was scheduled to pitch the fourth game, and he was determined to do just that. Despite his injury, he hit a fourth-inning triple that drove in two runs and gave Boston a 2–0 lead. He also shut out the Cubs for seven innings, but his sore hand began throbbing in the 8th, and the Cubs tied the game with two runs of their own. The Red Sox came back with another run to go ahead, 3–2.

When Ruth walked the first two batters in the 9th inning, manager Ed Barrow brought in a relief pitcher who saved the win. It was Ruth's third World Series victory without a defeat. He had shut out National League teams for $29\frac{2}{3}$ straight innings, besting Hall of Famer Christy Mathewson's record of 28.

Ruth's mark would stand for 43 years. Although he became famous all over the world for his great hitting, he was a pitcher at heart, and this record meant more to him than any of his others.

2

"I WAS A BUM"

Young George Ruth with his mother. This is the only known photograph of Ruth as a baby.

George Herman Ruth, Jr., was born on February 6, 1895, in a second-floor bedroom of his grandfather's house in Baltimore, Maryland. His parents lived upstairs over the saloon they operated a few blocks away. His mother had trudged through a blizzard to her parents' house to have her first child. Seven other children followed, including two sets of twins, but only George and his sister Mary lived past childhood.

The Ruth home was one room wide and two rooms deep. When young George entered his grandfather's house after exploring the narrow alleyways of the neighborhood, he came into a parlor about 12 feet wide. Behind it was a kitchen with a fireplace for cooking and a round dining table. Beside the fireplace, a narrow winding staircase led to the second- and third-floor bedrooms.

The brick house at 216 Emory Street still stands on a narrow lane near the waterfront. It is now the Babe Ruth Museum.

The Baltimore waterfront bustled with activity. Ships from all over the world docked there, and flocks of sailors filled the streets. From a window in their rooms above the saloon, George and his sister could watch the trains pulling up at a warehouse on the corner. The very spot where their home stood is now patrolled by centerfielders in the Baltimore Orioles' new ballpark.

While youngsters on farms were learning to pitch by throwing rocks at milk pails and squirrels, George Ruth was tossing apples and eggs at truck drivers, swiping food from free lunch counters, and draining the last drops of beer and whiskey from glasses left on barroom tables.

"I was a bum when I was a kid," he once admitted.

George, Sr., and his wife, Kate, worked long hours and had little time or energy to supervise young George. As his sister Mary later recalled, "My mother ordered me to make sure he attended school. But the truant officer spent more time at our house than his own. I swear I don't know how Babe did it. We had separate boys' and girls'

school yards, and we were not supposed to go into the other yard. I would sneak in to make sure he was there, and I'd even see him close the school door behind him. But somehow he always got out."

In every city at the turn of the century, there were institutions that took in both delinquents whose families could not control them and children from homes where there was not enough to eat. St. Mary's Industrial School for Boys, on the outskirts of Baltimore, was one such place.

In 1902, Kate Ruth decided that St. Mary's was the best place for her wayward son, and on June 13th, she legally turned George's custody over to them. For the next 12 years, he lived at St. Mary's. There he found clean clothes, three wholesome meals a day, regular classroom hours, and, most important, people who took an interest in his welfare every hour of the day. Each boy learned a trade, and George took up tailoring and shirtmaking. Years later, he would use his mother-in-law's sewing machine to fix the cuffs and collars on his shirts.

George left the school five times, when his

mother decided she missed him and wanted him at home. But each time he fell into his old ways and returned to St. Mary's. His mother died when he was 17.

St. Mary's was not a prison. There were no physical barriers preventing a boy from walking away from the school. But those who did had to face Brother Matthias when they returned. And Brother Matthias was a force to be reckoned with. A giant of a man, six and a half feet tall, he was stern yet kind, inspiring awe and respect.

George was not transformed into an angel at the school. In fact, he played practical jokes, sneaked cigarettes, and sometimes wandered off on his own. For the most part, however, Brother Matthias channeled George's energy into baseball. There were 800 boys at St. Mary's, and 43 teams. The teams played two or three games a day during the summer. Brother Matthias was the coach for all of them. He could flip a ball in the air and, swinging the bat with one hand, wallop it into the next pasture. That feat had a powerful impact on a young boy of the docks. George never forgot it—and he never met another man who could do the same.

Although George was a natural lefthander, Brother Matthias tossed him a righthander's catcher's mitt, and George wore it on his right hand. Despite that disadvantage, it soon became evident that George had extraordinary reflexes and coordination. He could hit a ball farther than any of the bigger, older boys.

George was very popular, especially with the younger kids. But he was still a wiseguy who had some lessons to learn. One day when the St. Mary's pitcher was being soundly whacked by the opposition, George started laughing and taunting him.

Brother Matthias immediately stopped the game. "If you think you can do better, George, let's see you go out there and pitch," he said.

George had no idea how to pitch, and he walked out to the mound reluctantly. But there he made a surprising discovery: he could throw the ball harder than any of the other kids.

With Brother Matthias's coaching, he learned the art of pitching: how to hold runners on base, and how to control the ball so it went where he wanted it to go. He pitched against other schools and was soon being touted in the Baltimore

"It was at St. Mary's that I met and learned to love the greatest man I've ever known," said Babe Ruth. "Matthias—Brother Matthias."

Wearing a tie and suit, 19-year-old George Herman Ruth signs his first professional contract. Baltimore Orioles owner Jack Dunn is seated, while standing is Ned Hanlon, the previous Orioles owner.

newspapers as a "schoolboy pitching star." George also played outfield or first base on occasion, and he turned out to be quite a star at the plate, too. One year, he hit 60 home runs in the more than 200 games he played.

When he was not playing ball, George pounded the big bass drum in the St. Mary's band and sang off-key in the choir. On the inside cover of his hymnal he wrote: "George H. Ruth, world's worse [sic] singer, world's best pitcher."

In the spring of 1913, the St. Mary's team traveled to Mount St. Joseph's for graduation ceremonies and a ball game. There George easily beat St. Joe's and moved a giant step closer to the world of professional baseball.

Jack Dunn was the owner-manager of the Baltimore Orioles in the International League. According to some stories, it was St. Joe's athletic director, Brother Gilbert, who tipped him off to Ruth, but Dunn may have read about the young pitcher's success in the newspaper. In any case, one February day in 1914, Dunn went to St. Mary's and spoke to Brother Matthias, who called George into his office and introduced him to Dunn. Then they went out to the icy field, and Dunn asked George to throw some pitches. After that, they went back inside. Brother Matthias told George that Dunn wanted him to play for the Orioles.

George had never considered baseball as a career, and Brother Matthias was uncertain about letting George leave the school. George was now 19, still legally a minor. After much thought, Brother Matthias signed the necessary papers, making Jack Dunn the teenager's official guardian. George's contract would pay him $600 for the season. In the meantime, Dunn handed him a five-dollar bill to spend on the train ride to spring training. It was the most money George had ever put in his pocket.

On February 27, 1914, George said goodbye to Brother Matthias and his friends at St. Mary's. "You'll make it, George," said the man who had taught him everything he knew.

George Ruth became idolized by people all over the globe, but he never forgot St. Mary's. Years later, when some of the school's buildings burned down, a great deal of money was needed for reconstruction. Ruth arranged for the St. Mary's band to tour American League cities with the Yankees and play concerts to raise money. He also bought Brother Matthias a new Cadillac every year and returned often to the school to play ball with the boys.

3

THE BABE
OF THE
BALLCLUB

The 1914 Baltimore Orioles. Ruth is at the far right, with his arm around his catcher, Ben Egan. Next to them (from right to left) are Jack Dunn; his son, Jack, Jr.; and Neal Ball, who made the first unassisted triple play in major-league history while playing shortstop for Cleveland in 1909.

He was George Ruth when the first train ride of his life brought him to Fayetteville, North Carolina, in March 1914. When he left a month later, he was Babe Ruth, or simply the Babe, and that is how he would be known from then on, even in places where few people had ever heard of baseball.

He was the butt of horseplay and practical jokes and the kind of razzing all young rookies endured in those days. But Jack Dunn had promised to keep a protective eye on him, and apparently he kept that promise. One day, a coach cautioned the veterans about George Ruth: "You'd better be careful," said the coach. "He's one of Dunn's babes." Ruth was the baby, or babe, of the camp after that.

Despite his youth, Ruth was already a complete player. He could hit the ball farther than anybody else in camp. And he knew how to pitch with the best of them—except for one thing. Young Babe Ruth had a habit of tipping his pitches by curling his tongue out of the corner of his mouth when he was bent on throwing a curve, but he was quickly cured of that.

Ruth's days with the Orioles ended almost as soon as they began, however. As a kid on the waterfront, George had never owned a bicycle. In Fayetteville, he saw the local boys riding bikes to the ballpark and thought it looked like fun. So he borrowed a bike and was soon pedaling all over the town. One day, he came tearing around a corner and just missed running over Jack Dunn. Braking violently and twisting the bike to one side, Ruth crashed into the back of a wagon and went down in a heap, with the bike on top of him. Ruth grinned sheepishly at Dunn, who glowered at him and said, "If you want to go back to the home, kid, just keep riding those bicycles."

Fortunately, Ruth was a lot more controlled on the field. When the Orioles played exhibition games against the best teams in the pre-season, Ruth did not seem to know one star from another. He had no fear of any batter, and he beat them all. As a hitter, the pitchers all looked alike to him, too.

According to Casey Stengel, who was an outfielder with the Dodgers at the time, "We had never heard of this kid. But they told me to play him way out in right field. I did and he hit one over my head. The next time he came up to bat I played out so far they could only see my cap sticking out from the tall grass. He hit another one over my head, farther than any human was supposed to hit a ball."

Soon after the 1914 season opened, Ruth made his first start for the Orioles, beating Buffalo, 6–0. The next day, he was sent up as a pinch-hitter and banged out a triple. Babe kept on winning and soon began attracting large crowds on the days he pitched.

All his life Ruth loved fast cars and fast bicycles.

Although the Orioles won 13 in a row and were in first place, they were losing money. Sometimes, there were only 150 people in the stands. A newly formed league, the Federal League, had built a new stadium right across the street from the Orioles' park. The F.L. was drawing all the fans, and Dunn knew he would have to sell some players to stay in business. He did not want to sell Ruth, but he had no choice.

Several teams expressed interest in the Babe, and the Boston Red Sox of the American League got him, along with pitcher Ernie Shore and catcher Ben Egan, on July 10, 1914.

Babe Ruth got off the train in Boston and went right to work. On July 11th, just 10 months after leaving St. Mary's, he started his first game for the Red Sox and beat the Cleveland Indians, 4–3. He struck out in his first at-bat, but that did not bother him. Throughout his career, he would strike out almost twice as often as he would hit a home run, but he never let it faze him. He might fan three or four times in a game and he would say, "That's okay. I'll get 'em tomorrow." And he usually did.

Ruth's confidence was not shared by his teammates, though. For the second time that year, he was a newcomer to a team.

"The Red Sox wanted no part of me, a busher," he recalled. "Because I like to hit and took my turn in batting practice with the regulars, I found all my bats sawed in half when I came to my locker the next day."

His teammates may not have given Ruth much of a welcome, but the Babe was not the least bit lonesome. Soon after he arrived in Boston, he fell in love with Helen Woodford, a waitress in his hotel's restaurant.

After losing his second start, Ruth was sent to the Sox's minor league team in Providence, Rhode Island. He came back in September, and on October 2nd got his first hit for the Sox, a double off King Cole of the Yankees. He finished the year with a combined 24–10 record for the three teams. Two weeks later, he and Helen were married. That winter, they lived with Ruth's father while Babe tended bar in the family tavern. Babe and Helen adopted a little girl, Dorothy.

Babe quickly established himself as a top pitcher who could also hit. Yet when he knocked out his first home run, on May 6, 1915, in New York, the newspapers took little notice of it. There were more important events to report: an American steamship, the *Lusitania*, had been sunk by a German submarine, bringing the war in Europe a little closer to home.

Ruth won 18 and lost 8 for the 1915 pennant-winning Red Sox, who had so many good pitchers they did not even need him to beat the Phillies in the World Series.

Had he not continued as a pitcher for the next three years, Ruth might have hit another 100 home runs and put his record beyond the reach of everybody. But he was about to become the best lefthander in the league, and he and the Red Sox saw his future as a pitcher.

The Red Sox edged the Chicago White Sox by two games to win the 1916 pennant. Ruth contributed 23 victories, and his 1.75 ERA was the best in the league. In the World Series, Ruth beat the Dodgers, 2–1, in the 14th inning, game 2, and the Red Sox went on to become world champions.

Ruth was almost as effective in 1917, with a 24–13 record, but this time the White Sox pushed Boston back into second place. Although there could be no doubt that Babe belonged in the majors, in some ways he was still the tough kid from the waterfront. On June 23, 1917, he blew up and helped his teammate Ernie Shore land a place in the record books. This is how it happened: Ruth started the game against the Washington Senators by walking the first batter on four pitches. Infuriated by the umpire's calls, he then marched over to home plate and socked the ump on the jaw. As a result, Ruth was thrown out of the game, and Shore came in to pitch. The base-

Ruth hit only 9 home runs in his first four years with the Red Sox. In 1918, he split his time between the outfield and the mound, and tied for the league lead in homers with 11.

runner was thrown out trying to steal, and Shore set down the next 26 batters in order. Shore was given credit for pitching a perfect game, while Babe was given a 10-day suspension.

Babe's public personality was beginning to emerge. The more celebrity he gained, the more his habits were embellished by the press. He was still growing, and one thing that was not exaggerated was his appetite for food. Whatever anybody else ordered for a meal, Ruth had doubles or triples. He ate steaks and chops for breakfast, could down 18 eggs and 3 slabs of

Ruth and Herb Pennock, two of the aces of the Red Sox staff. Ruth was sold to the Yankees in 1920 and Pennock was traded to New York in 1923. Between December 1918 and May 1925, the Yankees acquired 20 players, mostly first-stringers, from the Boston Red Sox.

ham in one sitting, and did not hesitate to devour a few pounds of raw hamburger for a snack. A gallon of ice cream was about right for him. He ate and drank very little before a game, maybe a sandwich and a bottle of milk. On doubleheader days, however, he would eat four or five hot dogs between games, then ask the trainer for "a little bi"—bicarbonate of soda—to soothe his stomach for the second game.

In the war-shortened 1918 season, Ruth was 13–7 and hit .300. The Red Sox won another pennant and their third World Championship in four years, beating the Cubs, 4 games to 2, in the Series.

Earlier that season, Boston captain Harry Hooper had noticed that attendance soared whenever Ruth pitched. The Red Sox had other fine hurlers, so he figured it was Ruth's batting and not his pitching that was drawing the fans. In one game, Babe got five hits, including three doubles and a triple.

Afterward, Hooper went up to manager Ed Barrow and said, "We need outfielders, not pitchers. We think the fans come out to see Ruth hit, so why not put him in the outfield every day?"

Barrow refused. "I would be the laughing-stock of the league if I took the best pitcher in the league and put him in the outfield."

But Hooper kept after him, and the manager finally relented. In 1919, Ruth played 111 games in the outfield and batted .322. He pitched in 17 games for a 9–5 record. All told, he led the league with 114 RBIs and 29 home runs (the rest of the Red Sox hit only 4 altogether). Nobody had ever hit so many homers, and few believed it could be done again.

Playing the outfield and pitching was hard

work, and Ruth complained that he was getting tired. The manager looked at the big, strong athlete, who was known for the late hours he kept.

"Of course, you're tired," Barrow barked. "That's because you're running around all the time. If you stopped your carousing at night and took better care of yourself, you could play every day and not feel it."

Barrow often worried that his players did not get enough sleep. On the road, he would sit in the hotel lobby until the whole team was in for the night. But he soon found himself losing sleep waiting up for Ruth. One night in Washington, Barrow asked the porter to call him when Babe Ruth returned.

At 6:00 A.M. there was a knock on his door. "That fellow just came in," the porter said.

Barrow put on his robe and slippers and walked down the hall to Ruth's room. He opened the unlocked door and found Ruth lying innocently in bed, smoking a pipe, the covers pulled up under his chin. His roommate had ducked into the bathroom.

"Do you always smoke a pipe at this time of the morning?" Barrow asked.

"Oh, sure, it's very relaxing," Ruth replied.

Barrow grabbed the covers and pulled them back, revealing Ruth still fully dressed, shoes and all.

That afternoon, the manager called a team meeting to discuss training rules, aiming most of his talk at Ruth. The Babe took it for a while, then threatened to punch Barrow in the nose. But when Barrow offered to take him up on the challenge, Ruth quietly got dressed and went out on the field with the other players. Barrow suspended him.

For the rest of his days as a player, Babe Ruth continued to ignore training rules and curfews, and he was sometimes fined and suspended for it. But he seemed immune from the effects that such bad habits would have had on ordinary mortals. He could party all night and still hit two home runs the next afternoon.

Despite Ruth's super season, Boston finished in sixth place. Red Sox owner Harry Frazee was also a producer of Broadway shows, and he was losing money in both endeavors. To solve his financial problems, he sold the best property he had—Babe Ruth—to the New York Yankees for a reported $125,000 and a big loan. Baseball fans in Boston still have not forgiven him, but it was a great deal for everyone else concerned. It turned the Yanks into perennial world champs and made Babe Ruth into America's biggest star.

5

START OF A DYNASTY

Babe Ruth's debut with the New York Yankees gave no hint that the team's fortunes and the entire game of baseball were about to change forever. On Opening Day, he dropped a fly ball that cost his new team a 3–1 loss to Philadelphia. The next day, he struck out three times, once with the bases loaded.

Babe Ruth did not hit a home run until May 1st, but after that nothing was ever the same. Ruth hit an astounding 54 home runs in 1920, more than any other *team* in the league, and he followed that with an unbelievable 59 in 1921. He batted .377 for the two years, and his slugging averages of .847 and .846 have never been equaled. He quickly became the most feared batter in the game, drawing a league-leading 148 walks in 1920. He would lead the league in walks 11 times as more and more pitchers opted to give him a free pass.

Ruth used a heavy bat—52 ounces. Most bats today weigh about 32. He was strong enough to swing it and believed the heft of the bat made

Babe Ruth attracted a crowd wherever he went.

the ball travel farther. He also gripped it as tightly as a drowning man squeezing a lifeline. "I try to make mush of the handle," he once said. "The harder you grip the bat, the faster the ball will travel."

Some pitchers foiled the Babe by throwing nothing but slow breaking stuff. He would get so frustrated he would yell at them to put something on the ball. But generally the scouting reports advised the men on the mound to do one thing: throw inside so Ruth might not hit it back through the middle, where it could hit the pitcher and injure him.

Off the field, however, it was Ruth who seemed more likely to be injured. Babe took to the automobile the way he had to his first bicycle. Driving fast and loose, he left many a car in a ditch. On July 7, 1920, it was rumored that he had been killed when his car ran off the road near Wawa, Pennsylvania. But Babe climbed jauntily out of that wreck. Over the years, he would survive many other mishaps behind the wheel. He was once arrested for going 42 miles per hour in New York City, fined $100, and sentenced to one day in jail. But the Yankees were playing that day, so the police released him early and gave him an escort to the game, where he arrived just in time for the sixth inning.

Beginning in 1921, Babe and the Yankees went on a rampage, winning six pennants and three World Series in eight years.

When the Yankees boarded a train, there would be racks of barbecued ribs or boxes of fried chicken and gallons of ice cream, all ordered and paid for by Ruth. This was just extra fare, to go along with whatever the dining car had to offer.

The Yankees lost the 1921 and 1922 World

Series to the rival Giants, who were then based in New York. During the 1922 season, Ruth missed some action because he was sick for a while with the flu and was suspended 30 days for violating the commissioner's ban on barnstorming. He still managed a more than respectable .315 average and 35 home runs, but in the 1922 World Series he batted a lowly .118. The newspapers blamed his poor performance on his being out of condition and criticized him soundly for it. At a dinner that winter, Jimmy Walker, later the mayor of New York, made a speech in which he chastised Ruth for letting down the dirty-faced kids on the streets of New York. According to one reporter, "The Babe arose with tears rolling down his face. He apologized to the writers and the kids, and promised to be good."

The Giants, led by John McGraw, had long

Opening Day, April 18, 1923, at the new Yankee Stadium, "The House That Ruth Built."

been the most successful and popular team in town. The Yankees were then playing their home games in the Giants' ballpark, the Polo Grounds. But as the attention and publicity shifted to Ruth, a resentful McGraw kicked them out. The Yankees were ready to build their own stadium anyway. They proceeded to put up Yankee Stadium, the most magnificent ballpark in the country, just across the Harlem River from the Polo Grounds. It was a theater built for Ruth, and it would be paid for many times over by the fans who flocked there to see the legendary Babe. In fact, it became known as "The House That Ruth Built."

In the spring of 1923, Babe was once again sidelined by the flu. His weight dropped to 200 pounds. Feeling weak and drained of all strength,

Ruth was never too busy to spend time with youngsters.

he began to wonder if he was already over the hill at 28. But all doubts disappeared when he led the gala opening ceremonies at the new Yankee Stadium on April 18, 1923. With two men on base, Ruth hit a home run to beat the Red Sox 4–1. By the end of the season, he had belted out a league-leading 41 home runs, drawn a record 170 walks, and batted a career-high .393. His on-base percentage reached .542. The Yankees won their third straight pennant, and this time they triumphed over the Giants for the championship, with Ruth hitting three home runs in the Series.

Babe was back on top, the toast of the town. He had already made his first movie, an epic about a ballplayer, called *Heading Home.* Now he went on a theater tour. First, there was film clip of him hitting a home run, and then he walked on stage, climbed up a platform, and swung at a ball hanging from a string. One day, he swung so mightily that he fell into the orchestra pit, scattering musicians and instruments with a loud clatter.

Ruth's looks were almost as dramatic as his actions. Most big leaguers of his era wore suits and ties and felt hats with the brim down. You could pick them out in a crowd; they were all well dressed and neatly groomed. Babe had reluctantly gone along with the style, though he thought he looked silly with a hat perched atop his large round head and full-moon face. Now that he was a star, he quit wearing hats and began sporting a flat camel's-hair cap wherever he went. It was not the fashion, but he no longer cared. It was his style, and he was in a class by himself.

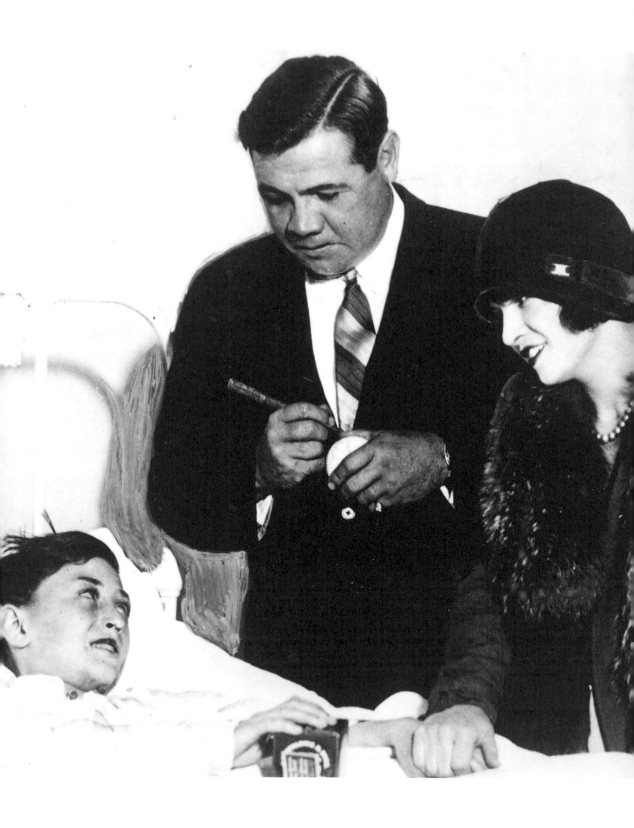

6

THE CROWD PLEASER

Everybody liked the Babe, including players on rival teams. He was a happy man who invited the affection of others. In many ways, he was like a big child, innocent and full of joy, playing a game he loved.

Wherever Babe went, a swarm of kids followed in his wake, scrambling to get close enough to touch him. But the Babe never complained about the loss of privacy that came with fame. And he never tried to duck his fans. Not Babe Ruth. He loved every minute of it. He became instant pals with all the kids, grinning and having as good a time as any of them.

The Babe's most publicized young pal was Johnny Sylvester, an 11-year-old boy who was bedridden with a bone disease brought on by a horseback riding accident. As Ruth remembered it, a man who worked for Johnny's father arranged for the two 1926 World Series teams to send Johnny signed baseballs to cheer him up. Ruth sent along a note: "I'll hit a home run for you in

Ruth signs a ball for bedridden Johnny Sylvester. It was for young Johnny that the Babe promised to "hit a homer" in 1926.

Wednesday's game." Ruth then went out and hit not one but three that day. Two weeks later, Babe went to see Johnny in person.

One time, when Ruth was driving home with his family after a long hot doubleheader, they stopped at a red light near a park where some boys were playing ball. The kids recognized Ruth and immediately crowded around the car.

"Come on, let's see you hit a few," they begged.

Ruth, who had already changed into white flannels and a silk shirt, got out and for 30 minutes hit some easy ones for the kids to catch and a few long balls over everybody's head while his family sat in the car.

Of course, the Babe saved his really long ones for the Yankees, hitting 46 homers in 1924. But even though he led the league with a .378 batting average, Washington took the pennant that year.

Then, in the spring of 1925, Ruth's world came crashing down. His weight ballooned above 250 pounds, and the newspapers were full of stories about the super slugger's decline. He reported to spring training still sick from his annual bout with the flu. When the Yankees arrived at Asheville, North Carolina, for an exhibition game, Babe collapsed in the railroad station, and the team went on without him. After a few days of rest, he felt better and headed for New York, but this time he fainted on the train. When it reached New York, he was rushed to the hospital in an ambulance. Rumors of his death flew around the world.

Weakened by an operation and a long stay in the hospital, Ruth missed the beginning of the 1925 season. His batting average slumped to .290, and he hit just 25 home runs as the Yankees tumbled to seventh place.

Although he seemed unable to regain his top condition, Ruth soon found the energy to resume his late-night activities—much to the displeasure of Yankees manager Miller Huggins. One day in St. Louis, Huggins decided he had had enough; he suspended Ruth and slapped a $5,000 fine on him. Babe went over the manager's head and complained to the club owner, but the owner backed Huggins. The fine stuck, and Ruth was not allowed back into the lineup until he apologized to Huggins.

That winter, ashamed of his part in the Yan-

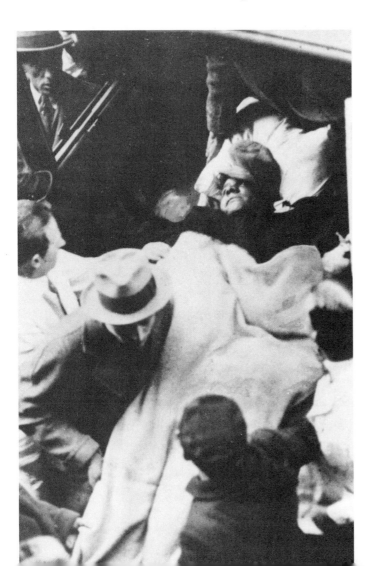

"The bellyache heard round the world." On April 9, 1925, Ruth is lifted into an ambulance, which will take him to New York's St. Vincent's Hospital.

Ruth, along with catcher Muddy Ruel and umpire Bill Dineen, watches home run number 60 leave the park. The pitcher was Tom Zachary of the Washington Senators.

kees' sad showing, Ruth vowed: "I'm going to make good all over again. I used to get sore when people called me a sap and tried to steer me right.... But all those people were right. Now, though, I know that if I am to wind up sitting pretty on the world I've got to face the facts and admit that I have been the sappiest of the saps."

Ruth was 31 years old at the time, and many people doubted that he really could come back. But Ruth was determined. All winter, he worked out every day in a gym. He even went on a diet and made sure he got plenty of sleep. Slowly, the weight melted away and his muscles hardened. Best of all, when the 1926 spring training began, no flu bug knocked him down.

The Yankees had three young players, including two rookies, in the infield that year—Lou Gehrig, Tony Lazzeri, and Mark Koenig—and nobody expected them to finish better than fourth. But the young Yanks went on to win the pennant by three games over the Indians. Ruth was a major factor in that winning season. He belted 47 home runs with 145 RBIs and a .372 batting average. In the World Series, he hit four

home runs, but the St. Louis Cardinals edged out New York in a seven-game battle.

The 1927 Yankees are generally considered the greatest team ever. They won 110 games, then a league record, and Ruth broke his own home-run record by hitting 60. That accounted for one-eighth of all the home runs hit in the American League that year. The Yankees averaged more than six runs per game and wound up 19 games ahead of second-place Philadelphia. They finished off the Pirates in four straight in the World Series.

New York repeated as champions in 1928 and this time swept the Cardinals in four, with Ruth hitting three homers and batting a record .625 in the Series.

Ruth was more than just a great hitter and pitcher. He was a fierce competitor, a smart baserunner, and an outstanding fielder. He had a strong, accurate arm and never made a mistake. He made errors, but he was rarely guilty of poor judgment, such as throwing to the wrong base. And he used his head. One day when he was playing left field, there was a man on second

Ruth gives some pointers to 22-year-old rookie Lou Gehrig in 1925. Together, the two sluggers were the most potent pair of home run hitters in the history of baseball.

with one out. A long fly was hit to left. Babe went back to the wall, turned, and looked up as if the ball were going into the seats. Then, as the man on second casually loped toward third, Ruth caught the ball and fired it to second for a double play.

Roger Maris hit more than 60 home runs in one year. Hank Aaron hit more than 714 career homers. Whitey Ford pitched more than $29\frac{2}{3}$ shutout innings in World Series play. But nobody else ever did it all the way Babe Ruth did.

Every man in baseball was in awe of the Babe and was thrilled to receive a hello and a few encouraging words from him. During batting practice, few players could resist stopping to watch when Ruth stepped in to take his cuts.

To understand the magnetism of Babe Ruth, you have to imagine a world without television, with radio stations just beginning to go on the air. Movies had no sound. People relied on newspapers for details of the games and photographs of the players. Thousands stood in the streets of cities and towns all across the country to watch World Series games recreated on huge electric display boards, while a man with a megaphone announced what was happening.

There were no big-league teams west of Chicago and St. Louis or south of Washington, D.C. The only chance people in those parts of the country had to see major leaguers play was in exhibition games played by clubs traveling home from spring training, or touring teams of stars in the off-season.

Waite Hoyt, Ruth's close friend on the Yankees, recalled, "I've seen them, fans driving miles in open wagons through the prairies of Oklahoma to see him in exhibition games as we headed north in the spring. I've seen them: kids, men, women, worshippers all, hoping to get his famous name on a torn, dirty piece of paper, or hoping for a grunt of recognition when they said, 'Hiya, Babe.' He never let them down, not once. He was the greatest crowd pleaser of them all."

Many such games were cut short when the crowd could no longer restrain itself and the fans ran out on the field to mob their hero. They did not care about the game or the score. They had come to see the great Babe Ruth.

7

THE LAST STARBURSTS

Babe Ruth's wife, Helen, did not share his love for public life, and she spent most of her time at their farm. It was there that she died in a terrible fire one night in January, 1929. On April 17, 1929, Babe married Claire Hodgson, an actress. Unlike his first marriage, this wedding made headlines all over the world. Although the ceremony was held before 6:00 A.M. to avoid a crowd, the church was filled and thousands of people waited outside to greet the newlyweds. They had a small wedding breakfast: only family and friends and every reporter and photographer in New York showed up. April 17th was Opening Day at Yankee Stadium, but it rained all day. So the Babe had to wait a day to hit a home run and doff his cap to his new bride as he circled the bases.

Claire Ruth had been married before, and like Ruth, she had a young daughter. Although the public made great demands of his time, Babe managed to be at home as much as he could. His

Mr. and Mrs. Ruth, shortly after they were married before 6 A.M. on April 17, 1929.

wife and daughters understood that he was a public figure with many outside interests tugging at him and made the most of the time he spent with them. When the girls were old enough to have boyfriends and go out on dates, they had an unusual problem: they could never be sure if the boys were really interested in them or were coming around to meet Babe Ruth.

In 1929, the Yankees began to put numbers on the backs of their uniforms, according to the batting order. Ruth, who batted third in the lineup, wore the number 3.

Near the end of that season, Miller Huggins died suddenly. Despite the hard time he had given the little manager, Ruth was as broken up as if he had lost his own father. Babe was now 34, and he was hoping to be named the Yankees' new manager. But former pitcher Bob Shawkey was chosen instead. The next year, Shawkey was fired and Ruth's hopes rose again. But this time Joe McCarthy got the job. Ruth resented McCarthy from the start and never tried to get along with him. It was nothing personal, simply a belief on Ruth's part that the manager's job should have been his. But even though the Yankee owner loved the Babe, he felt that Ruth had never managed himself well enough to indicate that he could manage a team of 25 players.

The Philadelphia Athletics dominated the American League from 1929 through 1931, but Babe was still king of the sluggers. He hit home run number 500 on August 11th, 1929, and number 600 two years and ten days later.

In 1932, the advancing years—and pounds—seemed to catch up with Babe Ruth. His knees, which had been injured in 1919, now ached constantly, and he had to wrap them in a heating pad every night. For the first time in seven years, he did not lead the league in home runs. A powerhouse named Jimmie Foxx out-homered him. But even an over-the-hill Babe Ruth was good enough for a .341 batting average and 137 RBIs to go with his 41 homers. The Yankees roared back to the top, 13 games ahead of the Athletics to win another A.L. pennant.

The Yankees faced the Cubs in the World Series. Although ex-Yankee shortstop Mark Koenig had helped Chicago win the pennant, the Cubs had not voted him a full share of the Series money. Ruth roasted the Cubs loudly, calling them "cheapskates," and the Cubs roared back at him with a lot worse. The Babe was waiting for his first turn at bat in game 3, exchanging insults with some of the Cubs, when he suddenly stopped in mid-sentence. Without another word,

In the 1932 World Series, Ruth receives congratulations from Gehrig after hitting the most celebrated home run in history. Did he or did he not call his shot? In 1945, Ruth said, "I didn't exactly point to any spot, like the flagpole. Anyway, I didn't mean to. I just sort of waved at the whole fence. All I wanted to do was give that ball a ride." Gehrig followed with a home run of his own.

Babe Ruth's 1934 Goudey gum card, the most valuable card in the set.

he pointed to right field and went up and hit a home run there. When he came to bat in the fifth inning with the score tied, 4–4, the Cubs really blasted him. This time Ruth pointed to pitcher Charlie Root and hollered, "Come on, pitch that ball and I'll knock it down your throat." And then he hit a long home run into the center field seats. This is the legendary blast that later became known as Ruth's "called shot." But Ruth had not been pointing to the outfield at that time, and his motion indicating he would hit one out in the first inning has somehow been forgotten. Most of the players who were there say he pointed at the Cubs' bench and then at their pitcher before he hit the second one. But it does not really matter whether he actually called that home run. It was heroic enough that he stood up to the scorching abuse he was taking in front of a large, hostile crowd at Wrigley Field and delivered the blows that defeated them.

The Yankees went on to sweep the Cubs, the third straight time they won a Series without losing a game. It turned out to be Babe Ruth's last World Series.

In 1933, the first All-Star Game was played, and Ruth hit a home run to give the American League a 4–2 victory. And on the last day of the 1933 season, Babe Ruth went back to his first love, pitching. He was 38 then, and although he had not pitched for three years, he faced the Red Sox and shut them out for the first five innings. His arm stiffened, but he pitched the whole game. He also hit the game-winning home run. But because of his stiff arm, he could not lift his left hand high enough to tip his cap to the crowd that waited for him an hour after the game ended, 6–5.

Still ailing, Babe was back in 1934—and

more popular than ever. His drawing power at the gate made him the highest paid player of the day. The nation was then deep in the Great Depression, and millions of people were out of work and hungry. But when Babe Ruth held out for more money, nobody criticized him. The New York *Sun* reported that Ruth earned more than a Supreme Court judge, college president, or state governor, but added that none of them "ever made 30,000 Americans spring up as one man in a delirium of delight. Thrill us and make us forget yesterday and tomorrow for a moment and you can name your own price."

Babe made a lot of money, but he spent it freely. He was a huge tipper, sometimes leaving $100 after a meal. He was a soft touch for loans, most of which were not repaid. Players would come up to him and say, "Lend me some money till payday," and the Babe would pull out a roll of big bills, peel some off, and never write anything down. When payday came around, some of the borrowers would hand him a $10 or a $50 bill and say, "Here's the money I owe you." The Babe never said a word.

Once, when a spring training game was rained out, Ruth went to the racetrack and won about $9,000. In those days, players did not get paid during spring training, and most of them were flat broke. Babe walked into the clubhouse, threw the whole wad of money on top of the equipment trunk, and said, "Well, boys, look what I found."

THE FINAL
SWING

In 1934, Babe Ruth's face was everywhere, in newspapers and magazines. A candy company wanted to name a candy bar for him, but there was already one called Baby Ruth, named for the daughter of President Grover Cleveland, so the idea was dropped.

Babe's popularity was at its height even as his ability was declining. In 125 games in 1934, he batted .288 and hit just 22 home runs as the Yankees finished second in the A.L. At the end of the season, a reporter asked the 39-year-old superstar if he would be back with the Yankees in 1935. "I won't play for them unless I can manage, too," Ruth replied.

The Yankees had no place for him in management, but they could not just let him go. It was

In ceremonies on June 13, 1948, marking the 25th anniversary of Yankee Stadium, the Babe's famous number, 3, was retired. Ruth was given the number in 1929, when the Yankees put numerals on the uniforms to match the player's spot in the lineup. Ruth was given number 3 because he batted third.

an awkward problem for them until the Boston Braves came up with a seemingly perfect solution. A mediocre team, the Braves badly wanted Ruth as a gate attraction. They made him a lot of promises, while hinting that he might one day take over as manager. The Babe signed with them. Few of the promises were kept, however, and it was an unhappy situation for Ruth and the Braves manager, Bill McKechnie.

Babe still drew the crowds, especially back in Boston. But after playing fewer than 30 games in the outfield, he declared that he was tired and wanted to quit. But the Braves had announced that Ruth would make one more swing around the rest of the league, and every city had declared its own Babe Ruth Day. The Babe was not one to disappoint the fans, so off he went for a long goodbye.

In Pittsburgh, he had a final day of glory. On Saturday, May 25th, he hit a home run in the first inning, another in the third, a single in the fifth, and still another homer—this one sailing out of the park and into the street—in the seventh. Altogether, he accounted for six RBIs.

Ruth would have been happy to bow out after that triumphant performance. Weary and sore, he could no longer reach balls hit near him in the outfield. But there were still two cities left on the trip. At Cincinnati the next day, he struck out three times. The last stop was Philadelphia, where a Memorial Day doubleheader was scheduled. Again, Ruth did not feel like playing, but a big crowd had come out to see him. After batting once, he trudged off the field and into the Phillies clubhouse. The trainer, Red Miller, asked if he could do anything for him.

"No," said the Babe. "There's nothing you can

do for old age. I had too many good days to have it end on a bad day like this."

And he never played again. Except for a brief stint as a coach for the Brooklyn Dodgers in 1938, that was the end of Babe Ruth's big-league career. He asked to be reinstated on the active list that year, but he had trouble seeing a pitch coming toward him, and for his own welfare he was turned down. For a while, Ruth's only connection with baseball was as a spectator. Whenever he was spotted in a box at Yankee Stadium, he drew a bigger hand than anybody on the field.

In 1941, America began fighting in World War II and millions of able-bodied young men joined the armed forces. Ruth appeared in exhibition games and other special events to raise money for war charities. In 1942, the Yankees organized an Army-Navy Relief Fund night. To

Ruth crosses home plate at spacious Braves Field in Boston after hitting his 710th home run, on April 21, 1935.

The United State Postal Service issued a stamp on July 6, 1983, honoring Babe Ruth.

guarantee a big turnout, they asked Ruth if he would try to hit one out against another star of yesteryear, Walter Johnson. The Babe agreed, and before the game he was as excited and fussy and anxious as if it were his debut. A big crowd was expected, and he did not want to disappoint them.

The crowd was big indeed—69,136—and Babe definitely did not disappoint them. After scattering 20 pitches to all parts of the field, he drove one into the third deck of the right-field stands.

Ruth continued to raise money for the war by playing golf exhibitions, and he became active in establishing the Babe Ruth League for teenage players.

Then the Babe got a sore throat, and his voice became hoarse. The doctors' diagnosis was cancer. From then on, Babe was in and out of the hospital. Although he was not allowed many visitors, nothing could stop the flood of get-well wishes that poured in from all over the world. A movie was made of his life, and he went to see the opening but was too sick to stay to the end.

In 1948, baseball celebrated a Babe Ruth Day in every ballpark. In New York, they retired his number, 3, and Ruth got out of his sickbed to be there. As he slowly made his way through the damp whitewashed underground corridors leading to the dugout, it was clear that he could not have made it without someone on each side to support him. His clothes hung loose on his once mighty body. The tan flat cap looked out of place above his gaunt face.

Many of his old Yankee buddies were there, along with Ty Cobb, Tris Speaker, and other old-time greats. The radio broadcaster of the Yankees, Mel Allen, introduced Ruth, and the whoops and whistles and cheers seemed as if they would never subside. The old players all had lumps in their throat and tears in their eyes. They knew they were saying thanks and farewell to the greatest of them all.

Ruth had to be helped to the microphone. "There have been so many lovely things said about me," his gravelly voice squawked through the loudspeakers. "I'm glad I can be here to thank everyone."

And with that, the Babe went back through the dugout and the runway as if he were leaving home for the last time.

Babe Ruth knew he was dying, but he did not want to lie in a hospital bed waiting for the end. So in the spring of 1948 he went to Florida and made the rounds of the training camps. He sat on a bench in St. Petersburg, in his familiar tan cap and coat, leaning on a cane carved with the monogram GHR that identified most of his possessions. Though he rarely could place a player or recall a name, when asked what he remembered about any ballpark, he had no trouble remembering when and how far he had socked his longest homer there.

Soon he was back in the hospital, and there on August 16, 1948, the Babe died. But the best of Babe Ruth will always live on in the memories of all those who saw him swing a bat, and in the imaginations of those who never saw him, and are a little the poorer for it.

CHRONOLOGY

Feb. 6, 1895	Born in Baltimore, Maryland
June 13, 1902	Goes to live at St. Mary's Industrial School for Boys
Feb. 1914	Signs with Baltimore Orioles of International League
July 10, 1914	Sold to Boston Red Sox
July 11, 1914	Wins first major-league start, 4–3, over Cleveland
Oct. 2, 1914	Gets first major-league hit, a double
Oct. 17, 1914	Marries Helen Woodford
May 6, 1915	Knocks out first major-league home run
Sept.9, 1918	Sets World Series record, pitching 29⅔ straight shutout innings
1919	Hits record 29 home runs and is converted to outfielder
Jan. 6, 1920	Red Sox owner Harry Frazee sells Ruth to New York Yankees to finance Broadway production of *No, No, Nanette*
1920	Ruth hits record 54 home runs
1921	Hits record 59 home runs
Oct. 9, 1921	Hits first World Series homer
April 18, 1923	Hits home run in opening game at Yankee Stadium
Oct. 6, 1926	Hits three home runs in one World Series game
Sept. 30, 1927	Bests his own single–season record again with his 60th homer, setting a mark that would stand for 34 years
Oct. 9, 1928	Hits three home runs in one World Series game
Jan. 11, 1929	Helen Ruth dies in a fire
April 17, 1929	Marries Claire Hodgson
Aug. 11, 1929	Hits 500th home run
Aug. 21, 1931	Hits 600th home run
Oct. 1, 1932	Beats Chicago Cubs in game 3 of the World Series with famed "called shot" home run
July 13, 1934	Hits 700th home run
Feb., 1935	Yankees release Ruth and he signs with Boston Braves
May 25, 1935	Launches last three home runs at Pittsburgh for a lifetime total of 714 round trippers
June 13, 1948	Makes a final appearance in Yankee Stadium as Babe Ruth Day is celebrated in every major-league ballpark
Aug. 16, 1948	Dies of cancer in New York

GEORGE HERMAN (BABE) RUTH
BOSTON-NEW YORK, A.L.; BOSTON, N.L.
1915 - 1935
GREATEST DRAWING CARD IN HISTORY OF
BASEBALL. HOLDER OF MANY HOME RUN
AND OTHER BATTING RECORDS. GATHERED
714 HOME RUNS IN ADDITION TO FIFTEEN
IN WORLD SERIES.

MAJOR LEAGUE STATISTICS

BOSTON RED SOX, NEW YORK YANKEES, BOSTON BRAVES

YEAR	TEAM	G	AB	R	H	2B	3B	HR	RBI	BA	SB
1914	BOS A	5	10	1	2	1	0	0	0	.200	0
1915		42	92	16	29	10	1	4	21	.315	0
1916		67	136	18	37	5	3	3	16	.272	0
1917		52	123	14	40	6	3	2	12	.325	0
1918		95	317	50	95	26	11	11	66	.300	6
1919		130	432	103	139	34	12	29	114	.322	7
1920	NY A	142	458	158	172	36	9	54	137	.376	14
1921		152	540	177	204	44	16	59	171	.378	17
1922		110	406	94	128	24	8	35	99	.315	2
1923		152	522	151	205	45	13	41	131	.393	17
1924		153	529	143	200	39	7	46	121	.378	9
1925		98	359	61	104	12	2	25	66	.290	2
1926		152	495	139	184	30	5	47	145	.372	11
1927		151	540	158	192	29	8	60	164	.356	7
1928		154	536	163	173	29	8	54	142	.323	4
1929		135	499	121	172	26	6	46	154	.345	5
1930		145	518	150	186	28	9	49	153	.359	10
1931		145	534	149	199	31	3	46	163	.373	5
1932		133	457	120	156	13	5	41	137	.341	2
1933		137	459	97	138	21	3	34	103	.301	4
1934		125	365	78	105	17	4	22	84	.288	1
1935	BOS N	28	72	13	13	0	0	6	12	.181	0
Total		2503	8399	2174	2873	506	136	714	2211	.342	123
World Series											
(10 Years)		41	129	37	42	5	2	15	33	.326	4
All-Star Games											
(2 Years)		2	6	2	2	0	0	1	2	.333	0

PITCHING STATISTICS

YEAR	TEAM	W	L	PCT	ERA	G	GS	CG	IP	H	BB	SO	ShO
1914	BOS A	2	1	.667	3.91	4	3	1	23	21	7	3	0
1915		18	8	.692	2.44	32	28	16	217.2	166	85	112	1
1916		23	12	.657	1.75	44	41	23	323.2	230	118	170	9
1917		24	13	.649	2.01	41	38	35	326.1	244	108	128	6
1918		13	7	.650	2.22	20	19	18	166.1	125	49	40	1
1919		9	5	.643	2.97	17	15	12	133.1	148	58	30	0
1920	NY A	1	0	1.000	4.50	1	1	0	4	3	2	0	0
1921		2	0	1.000	9.00	2	1	0	9	14	9	2	0
1930		1	0	1.000	3.00	1	1	1	9	11	2	3	0
1933		1	0	1.000	5.00	1	1	1	9	12	3	0	0
Total		94	46	.671	2.28	163	148	107	1221.1	974	441	488	17
World Series													
(2 Years)		3	0	1.000	0.87	3	3	2	31	19	10	8	1

FURTHER READING

Allen, Lee. *Babe Ruth, His Story in Baseball.* New York: G.P. Putnam, 1966.

Creamer, Robert. *Babe, The Legend Comes to Life.* New York: Simon & Schuster, 1974.

Daniel, Dan & H.G. Salsinger. *The Real Babe Ruth.* St. Louis, MO: The Sporting News, 1963.

Eisenberg, Lisa. *The Story of Babe Ruth: Baseball's Greatest Legend.* New York: Dell-Yearling, 1990.

Meany, Tom. *Babe Ruth: The Big Moments of the Big Fellow.* New York: A.S. Barnes, 1947.

Pirone, Dorothy Ruth. *My Dad the Babe: Growing up with an American Hero.* Boston: Quinlan Press, 1988.

Ritter, Lawrence, and Mark Rucker. *The Babe: A Life in Pictures.* New York: Ticknor & Fields, 1988.

Ruth, Babe. *The Babe Ruth Story.* (As told to Bob Considine) New York: E.P. Dutton, 1948.

Smelser, Marshall. *The Life that Ruth Built.* New York: Quadrangle Press, 1975.

Sobol, Ken. *Babe Ruth & the American Dream.* New York: Random House, 1974.

Wagenheim, Kal. *Babe Ruth: His Life and Legend.* New York: Praeger, 1974.

Weldon, Martin. *Babe Ruth.* New York: Thomas Y. Crowell, 1948.

INDEX

PICTURE CREDITS

The Babe Ruth Museum: pp. 12, 14, 32; Courtesy of the Bronx County Historical Society Collection, Bronx, NY: p. 35; Culver Pictures: p. 2; Kenneth A. Felden: p. 28; National Baseball Library, Cooperstown, NY: pp. 8, 17, 18, 20, 23, 36, 42, 44, 46, 49, 52, 55, 58, 60; Photo File: p. 38; Courtesy of Larry Ritter: p. 41; Courtesy of Bert Randolph Sugar: p. 50; UPI/Bettmann: p. 26; Courtesy of U.S. Postal Service: p. 56

NORMAN MACHT was a minor league general manager with the Milwaukee Braves and Baltimore Orioles organizations and has been a stock broker and college professor. His work has appeared in *The BallPlayers*, *The Sporting News*, *Baseball Digest* and *Sports Heritage*, and he is the co-author with Dick Bartell of *Rowdy Richard*. Norman Macht lives in Newark, Delaware.

JIM MURRAY, veteran sports columnist of the *Los Angeles Times*, is one of America's most acclaimed writers. He has been named "America's Best Sportswriter" by the National Association of Sportscasters and Sportswriters 14 times, was awarded the Red Smith Award, and was twice winner of the National Headliner Award. In addition, he was awarded the J. G. Taylor Spink Award in 1987 for "meritorious contributions to baseball writing." With this award came his 1988 induction into the National Baseball Hall of Fame in Cooperstown, New York. In 1990, Jim Murray was awarded the Pulitzer Prize for Commentary.

EARL WEAVER is the winningest manager in Baltimore Orioles history by a wide margin. He compiled 1,480 victories in his 17 years at the helm. After managing eight different minor league teams, he was given the chance to lead the Orioles in 1968. Under his leadership the Orioles finished lower than second place in the American League East only four times in 17 years. One of only 12 managers in big league history to have managed in four or more World Series, Earl was named Manager of the Year in 1979. The popular Weaver had his number 5 retired in 1982, joining Brooks Robinson, Frank Robinson, and Jim Palmer, whose numbers were retired previously. Earl Weaver continues his association with the professional baseball scene by writing, broadcasting, and coaching.